The Oncology Interview questions

Strategies for Success: The Definitive Oncology Interview Companion: 50+ Interview Questions, Insights, and Sample Answers

Bonus: 20 Interview Tips

Michele C. Guevara

Copyright

Disclaimer

This guide's content is intended solely for general informational purposes. For specific medical or healthcare-related concerns, readers are advised to consult with licensed healthcare professionals. This information is not construed as professional advice. About the information contained herein, the author and publisher make no express or implied representations or warranties of any kind regarding its availability, suitability, accuracy, completeness, or reliability. The reader assumes all risks for using the information in this guide. Any liability for any loss or damage resulting from the use of this guide is disclaimed by the author and publisher.

About the Author

Renowned medical expert Michele C. Guevara is passionate about enhancing patient outcomes and developing healthcare. With a strong background in oncology, Michele has devoted her professional life to providing people with cancer with compassionate care.

Michele is a seasoned medical professional who brings a wealth of knowledge to her writing career. She draws from years of research, clinical experience, and education. Her strategic approach to oncology, which emphasizes empathetic communication, multidisciplinary collaboration, and the complex nuances of the field, demonstrates her commitment to excellence in patient care.

Apart from her clinical work, Michele is a passionate teacher who imparts her knowledge to aspiring medical professionals and other medical professionals. Her writing demonstrates her dedication to sharing knowledge and serves as a useful guide for individuals navigating the intricacies of oncology practice.

In addition to her professional achievements, Michele wants to use her work to encourage and mentor medical professionals to succeed in the demanding and fulfilling field of oncology.

Table of Content

How To Maximize This Book

To get the most out of "The Oncology Interview questions," it's essential to approach the book with a strategic mindset and use it as a comprehensive resource to enhance your interview preparation for roles in oncology. Here's a guide on how to maximize the benefits from the book:

❖ Thorough Reading and Understanding:

Begin by thoroughly reading the book from cover to cover. Familiarize yourself with the structure, key sections, and the overall flow of the content. This foundational step ensures you have a comprehensive understanding of the material.

❖ Identify Key Topics and Themes:

Pay attention to key topics and recurring themes throughout the book. These may include clinical scenarios, ethical considerations, patient communication strategies, and other relevant aspects of oncology interviews. Take notes on important points to facilitate later review.

❖ Interactive Learning:

Treat the book as an interactive learning tool. Engage with the content actively by jotting down your thoughts, answering reflection questions, and considering how the information applies to your own experiences or potential interview scenarios.

❖ Self-Assessment and Reflection:

Use the book as a self-assessment tool. Identify your strengths and areas that may need improvement based on the guidance provided. Reflect on your past experiences and consider how you can incorporate the book's insights into your own approach to oncology interviews.

❖ Practice Scenarios and Questions:

Take advantage of any practice scenarios or sample interview questions included in the book. Practice your responses to these questions, either on your own or with a peer, to build confidence and refine your communication skills in an oncology context.

❖ Application to Real-World Situations:

Apply the concepts learned from the book to real-world situations. Consider how you would approach challenging cases, communicate with patients and their families, and collaborate with other healthcare professionals. Relate the book's advice to your own professional experiences.

❖ Create a Personalized Interview Strategy:

Tailor the insights gained from the book to create a personalized interview strategy. Identify specific techniques and communication styles that resonate with you, and integrate them into your approach. Develop a plan that aligns with the book's recommendations and your own strengths.

❖ Continuous Reference and Revision:

Keep the book as a reference guide throughout your interview preparation journey. Periodically revisit key sections, especially those that focus on challenging aspects of oncology interviews. Use the book as a resource for ongoing revision and reinforcement of important concepts.

❖ Seek Additional Resources:

While "The Oncology Interview Questions" provides valuable information, consider supplementing your learning with additional resources. Explore recent research articles, case studies, and online forums to stay updated on the latest developments in oncology practice and interview strategies.

Introduction

Thank you for Purchasing 'The Oncology Interview Questions,' a thorough reference book created to assist medical professionals aiming to succeed in the difficult field of oncology. With its strategic approach to handling difficult situations, proficient patient and colleague communication, and navigating the multidisciplinary facets of cancer care, this book offers priceless insights into the complex world of oncology interviews. This guide is intended for oncologists of all experience levels to improve their performance in oncology-related interviews and raise their game.

1

What motivated you to work in oncology?

This is a question that a hiring manager might pose to you to learn more about your goals and areas of interest within oncology. They might learn more about your passion for your work and your personal and professional interests if they comprehend why you chose to pursue oncology. In your response, make sure to highlight how dedicated you are to your work. Describe your involvement and give a detailed explanation of your career decision in oncology. If appropriate, you could briefly describe how you became involved in cancer care from a personal perspective. Alternatively, you could concentrate on your career aspirations and sources of inspiration.

Sample Answer: I've always wanted to be a doctor, and when my sister was diagnosed with cancer at the age of 24, that's when my journey to become an oncologist began. Our family was going through a trying time, but her care team helped us feel supported as we went through the course of treatment. My desire to treat people with the same caliber of care was sparked by my interactions with so many wise and kind professionals. We were able to trust the doctors' expertise because they always made us feel welcome, took the time to explain treatment procedures to us, and answered our questions.

2

What do you think the oncology field will face as its largest challenge in the next ten years?

This is a question that interviewers may use to gauge your understanding of prospective and present problems in the field of oncology. You can discuss the causes of the issue and possible solutions by responding to this question, which also shows that you understand the issues the field may encounter. Give an example of a major problem and an explanation of why it is a problem when responding. You might also offer a solution to the problem and how you think your professional background in the field could help. This demonstrates your knowledge of the industry and your commitment to advancing it as a practitioner.

Sample Answer: I believe that the lack of qualified professionals will be our industry's biggest problem in the next ten years. The demand for oncologists may exceed the supply of working professionals due to the aging of the American population and the present low enrollment rates in medical schools. The current workforce may be under stress due to the shortage of providers, which could result in higher rates of burnout among practitioners and less effective patient treatments. To support doctors, I think we should invest more in oncology nurses, nurse practitioners, and physician assistants receiving specialized training in diagnosis and treatment methods to counteract this trend.

3

What, in your opinion, distinguishes oncology from other medical specialties?

This is a question that an interviewer might ask for a few different reasons. Assessing the oncologist's interest and expertise in the field of oncology is one reason. Career success is more likely for oncologists who have a strong understanding of the field and are enthusiastic about what they do. This question can also aid the interviewer in comprehending the reasons behind the oncologist's decision to work in the field. To determine how dedicated an oncologist is to their work, it's critical to understand why they selected this specialty. Lastly, asking the oncologist about their opinions on cancer care and treatment can also be helpful to the interviewer. Success in the workplace is more likely for oncologists who are dedicated to giving their patients the best care possible and who have a positive outlook on cancer treatment.

Sample Answer: The study and treatment of cancer is known as oncology. A variety of illnesses that can impact any area of the body are collectively referred to as cancer. Physicians who specialize in the diagnosis and treatment of cancer are known as oncologists.

Cancer can come in a variety of forms, and each one may respond differently to treatment. To design the most effective treatment plan for each patient, oncologists collaborate with other medical professionals like radiation therapists and surgeons.

Radiation therapy, chemotherapy, and surgery are frequently used in conjunction with the treatment of cancer. Immunotherapy, stem cell transplants, and targeted therapies are additional treatments that oncologists may employ to treat cancer.

4

In your opinion, what are the most critical attributes of an oncologist?

The interviewer is attempting to ascertain what attributes the oncologist thinks are critical for a person in their line of work. This is significant because it can reveal how the oncologist sees their work and what they think is necessary to be successful in their line of work. Understanding how the oncologist interacts with patients and whether they possess the bedside manner necessary for this kind of work can also be helpful to the interviewer.

Sample Answer: The following are the most crucial characteristics of an oncologist:

a. Compassion: To comprehend and empathize with their patients' experiences, oncologists need to possess compassion.

b. Communication abilities: To give their patients the best care possible, oncologists need to be able to communicate with them effectively.

c. Organizational abilities: To monitor the medical records and treatment regimens of their patients, oncologists need to be extremely organized.

d. Problem-solving abilities: To give their patients the best care possible, oncologists need to be able to recognize problems and find solutions.

5

How do you stay current with oncology advances?

Keeping up with oncology advancements is essential to giving cancer patients the best care possible. Medical oncologists must stay up to date on the most recent advancements in pharmaceuticals, treatment modalities, and research findings. This inquiry is meant to evaluate your dedication to lifelong learning and staying on the cutting edge of your profession, both of which contribute to improved patient care.

Sample Answer: It's imperative to stay current in the field of oncology." I make sure of this by frequently going to medical conferences and seminars, which offer up-to-date information on the newest findings and developments.

Additionally, I read several medical journals that publish the most recent research, including The

Lancet Oncology and the Journal of Clinical Oncology.

I can interact with other professionals in my field and promote knowledge exchange by taking part in professional networks and online forums.
Finally, I dedicate time to ongoing education by enrolling in recognized courses and training courses. I can stay on top of cancer advancements thanks to this all-encompassing approach.

6

Tell about an encounter you had with a challenging patient. What was your course of action?

The purpose of asking you this behavioral interview question is to find out how you handle difficult patients. Explaining your capacity for empathy toward patients dealing with serious health issues and your aptitude for meaningful patient communication should be the main emphasis of your response to this question. Give an example of a particular instance when you dealt with a difficult patient. Tell us about the circumstances and the background. Afterward, describe the actions you took to comprehend the patient's viewpoint, show empathy for their situation, and collaborate with them to find a solution.

Sample Answer: I once dealt with a patient who voiced serious worries about the safety and health effects of X-rays. I ordered an X-ray to look into a medical complaint, but she objected because she thought they caused illness. I spoke with her in private for a short while, listening to her concerns and reassuring her that her worries about her health were valid. I then spent some time explaining the studies on X-ray safety so she could decide what tests were best for her. She consented to the X-ray after the discussion.

7

Is there a scenario you would like to share about effectively managing a patient's pain?

Since it touches on one of the main duties of an oncologist, which is to manage a patient's pain, this is an important question. Answering this question will reveal information about your clinical expertise, decision-making process, and patient-interaction style. Furthermore, it will demonstrate to a prospective employer how you resolve conflicts between professionalism and empathy in challenging circumstances.

Sample Answer: I once saw a patient who had advanced lung cancer and was in excruciating pain. Even though she was taking opioids, there was little relief and a lot of side effects.

Developing an efficient pain management plan required me to work with a multidisciplinary team that included palliative care specialists. The amount of pain was greatly decreased when we implemented nerve blocks.

To best balance pain management with side effects, we also changed the dosage of opioids. We were able to modify the plan as necessary thanks to routine evaluations. Using this method during treatment helped the patient's quality of life.

8

What are the main obstacles that oncologists encounter, in your opinion?

An oncologist could be asked this question during an interview for a few different reasons. In the first place, it enables the interviewer to determine how well-versed the oncologist is in the difficulties their field faces. In addition, it gives the interviewer insight into the oncologist's perspective on the obstacles their field faces and their plans for overcoming them. Lastly, it enables the interviewer to gain insight into the oncologist's priorities and outlook on the field.

Sample Answer: Oncologists face three major challenges:

- How complicated cancer treatments are becoming: To provide their patients with the best care possible, oncologists must stay up to date with the latest developments in cancer treatments, which are becoming increasingly complex. With so much new information to remember, this can be difficult.

- Cancer treatments are expensive: Due to their high cost, many patients are unable to afford cancer treatments. From insurance coverage to patient affordability, oncologists occasionally have to make tough choices regarding recommended treatments.

- Cancer patients' emotional toll during treatment: Treatment for cancer patients and their families can be extremely emotionally taxing. The emotional strain of the job must be managed by oncologists to continue giving their patients the best care possible.

9

Which aspect of oncology, in your opinion, offers the greatest rewards?

One could ask an oncologist this question for a few different reasons during an interview. To find out if the oncologist is satisfied with their work could be one reason. Asking the oncologist to consider what they enjoy most about their job may also be a useful technique to get them to think about what drives them to perform this kind of work. It may also be possible to determine from this question which aspects of the patients' lives the oncologist feels they have the greatest influence or difference. In the end, determining the oncologist's degree of job satisfaction and commitment requires the interviewer to ascertain what aspects of their work they find most fulfilling.

Sample Answer: Helping patients and their families through some of the most trying times in their lives is one of the most satisfying aspects of oncology, but there are many other rewarding aspects as well. It's a deeply satisfying feeling for oncologists to be able to offer hope and support when it's most needed. It is also immensely fulfilling to witness cancer patients triumph over their illness and lead fulfilling lives.

10

Which cancer research developments do you consider to be the most significant?

To determine the oncologist's level of clinical expertise and knowledge; to learn more about the treatments the oncologist recommends or is most familiar with; and to learn about the oncologist's research interests, among other possible motives, an interviewer may pose this question to an oncologist. Examine the oncologist's knowledge of the most recent advancements in cancer research.

To give their patients the best care possible, oncologists must stay up to date on the most recent research findings in their field. Novel insights into cancer biology may yield novel therapeutic approaches and treatments that enhance prognoses for patients. Additionally, oncologists can improve their understanding of the disease process and discover possible new research areas by keeping up with the most recent research.

Sample Answer: Throughout the years, there have been numerous significant advancements in oncology research. Among the most significant are the ones listed below:

- ❖ The creation of efficient cancer therapies, like radiation therapy and chemotherapy
- ❖ Finding the genes and mutations that cause cancer
- ❖ The introduction of novel imaging modalities that aid in the detection and staging of cancer, like MRIs and PET scans
- ❖ The advancement of novel surgical methods that can enhance results, like minimally invasive surgery
- ❖ The discovery of new cancer risk factors, such as particular lifestyle decisions and environmental exposures.

11

In your opinion, what are the most pressing unfulfilled needs in oncology?

There exist several rationales for an interviewer to pose this query to an oncologist. It can first aid the interviewer in comprehending the oncologist's priorities and areas of concentration. Second, it can reveal to the interviewer how up-to-date the oncologist is on the most recent procedures and scientific advancements in the field. Lastly, it can assist the interviewer in determining how passionate the oncologist is about supporting cancer patients.

Sample Answer: There are a lot of unmet needs in oncology, from more efficient methods for cancer prevention and detection to better treatments for uncommon cancers. But among the most urgent unmet needs are the following:

- More potent therapies for metastatic and advanced cancer

- Enhancing strategies to avert cancer
- More potent therapies for uncommon cancers
- More potent therapies for pediatric cancers
- Better availability of high-quality cancer care

12

In your opinion, which oncology treatment area shows the most promise?

This question is probably being asked by the interviewer to gauge the oncologist's present opinion on the most effective courses of action for cancer patients. This is a crucial question because it lets the interviewer determine how knowledgeable and experienced the oncologist is in the field. This inquiry may also shed light on the oncologist's future research objectives.

Sample Answer: Immunotherapy is one of the most promising areas of treatment in oncology, but there are many promising areas. Immunotherapy is a medical intervention that targets cancer cells by stimulating the body's immune system. Although it is still in the early phases of research and development, it has demonstrated great promise in the treatment of numerous cancer types.

13

What do you believe to be the most significant obstacle currently facing cancer patients?

Today's cancer patients deal with many difficulties. The largest obstacle is getting access to care. A large number of cancer patients have inadequate or no insurance. This implies that they might not have the money to pay for the necessary medical care. It might also be difficult for them to locate a physician who will treat them. The consequences of treatment present another difficulty. It can be difficult for cancer patients to lead normal lives because of the pain, fatigue, and other side effects they frequently experience.

Sample Answer: The high cost of treatment is currently the largest obstacle facing cancer patients. Because cancer treatment is so costly, many patients are unable to pay for it. Furthermore, insurance frequently does not cover cancer treatments. Patients must now cover the cost of their care, which can be exceedingly challenging.

14

In your opinion, what can cancer patients do most effectively to increase their chances of survival?

Cancer patients who maintain a positive outlook, engage in regular exercise, and consume a healthy diet can increase their chances of survival.

Sample Answer: There is no one-size-fits-all response to this query because each cancer patient's situation will determine what is most crucial for increasing their chances of survival. Nonetheless, the following general advice might be helpful to all cancer patients:

- Give up smoking: Smoking lowers one's chances of surviving cancer and is one of the main risk factors for the disease. For your health, giving up smoking is the best thing you can do if you smoke.

- Eat a nutritious diet: Eating a nutritious diet can strengthen your immune system and provide your body with the resources it needs to combat cancer. A smart place to start is by eating an abundance of fruits, vegetables, and whole grains.

- Get regular exercise: Exercise offers many health benefits, such as lowering the risk of cancer and increasing the chances of survival for those who have already been diagnosed with the disease.

- Reduce alcohol intake: Alcohol consumption raises the risk of cancer, impedes the course of treatment, and lowers survival rates. It's crucial to use alcohol in moderation if you do.

- Decrease stress: Stress impairs immunity and increases the body's difficulty in fending off cancerous cells.

15

In your opinion, what are the most crucial actions that cancer patients and their loved ones can take to manage the illness?

Coping with cancer presents numerous challenges for patients and their families. The most crucial thing they can do is ask for help from friends, family, and experts who can guide them through the difficulties. Additionally, it's critical to maintain optimism and find coping mechanisms for stressful situations.

Sample Answer: Cancer patients and their families can do several crucial things to help them deal with the illness. Among the most crucial elements are:

❖ Taking up healthy habits, such as eating a balanced diet and exercising frequently.

❖ Healthy techniques for handling stress.

- ❖ Taking part in the selection of cancer treatments.

- ❖ Asking friends, family, and experts for assistance.

- ❖ Acquiring as much knowledge as you can about the illness.

- ❖ Having an optimistic outlook and maintaining hope.

- ❖ Looking for creative outlets to express feelings, like writing, painting, or music.

- ❖ Making connections with other cancer survivors to get motivation and support

16

In your opinion, what are the most crucial steps that cancer patients can take to stop the illness from coming back?

The interviewer is trying to get the oncologist's expert opinion on what cancer patients can do to keep the illness from coming back. This is a crucial question to ask because the answers can help cancer patients make decisions about their care and course of action.

Sample Answer: Cancer patients can take the following steps to stop the disease from coming back:

- Adopt a healthy lifestyle: Regular exercise, a balanced diet, and weight management can all help lower the chance of cancer reoccurring.

- Give up smoking - Since smoking is one of the main risk factors for cancer, giving up can help lower the chance that the illness will recur.

- Schedule routine checkups - By visiting a physician regularly, you can help detect cancer early on, when it is most curable.

17

In your opinion, what are the most crucial actions that cancer patients can take to enhance their quality of life following treatment?

Following treatment, cancer patients frequently see a reduction in their quality of life as a result of side effects like nausea, pain, and fatigue. The patient's quality of life may be enhanced by the oncologist's treatment recommendations or lifestyle adjustments.

Sample Answer: After treatment, cancer patients can do a lot to enhance their quality of life. Among the most crucial elements are:

- Maintaining a nutritious diet and abstaining from tobacco.

- Controlling stress and preserving mental well-being.

- Continuing to exercise and keeping a healthy weight.

- Attending routine medical examinations and screenings.

18

In your opinion, what are the most crucial things that relatives and patients with cancer can do to help one another through treatment?

Keeping lines of communication open is the most crucial thing cancer patients and their families can do to support one another during treatment. Maintaining open channels of communication is crucial to ensuring that everyone is informed and on the same page about what is going on. Everyone concerned will experience a decrease in stress and anxiety as a result of this. Establishing a support network, comprising friends, family, or a group dedicated to cancer patients and their families, is also beneficial. Having support systems during this trying time can be extremely beneficial.

Sample Answer: Cancer patients and their families can help each other out during treatment in a variety of ways. Among the most crucial actions they can take are:

a. Share their thoughts and feelings honestly and openly.
b. Spend time together, engaging in activities they enjoy or just conversing. You can also go for walks together.
c. Offer each other physical and emotional support.
d. Assist one another with household chores, cooking, cleaning, and traveling.
e. Support one another in maintaining optimism and holding out hope.

19

Could you give an example of a time when a patient's quality of life was considerably enhanced by your treatment plan?

Being a medical oncologist is about more than just curing illness; it's about enhancing a patient's quality of life. The purpose of a hiring manager's question is to gauge your commitment to patient-centered care. They want to know how you approach treatment plans, how kind you are, and how your choices have improved the lives of your patients.

Sample Answer: I remember a patient who had severe pain and dyspnea due to advanced lung cancer. The ineffectiveness of conventional chemotherapy had a major negative effect on her quality of life.

I considered her case and, based on the genetic profile of her tumor, I changed our course of treatment to targeted therapy. This method significantly reduced her symptoms in addition to shrinking her tumor.

She was able to breathe more easily, regain her strength, and resume her participation in family activities. Seeing how individualized care can significantly enhance a patient's quality of life was satisfying.

20.

How would you approach a patient who has been told they have terminal cancer in terms of discussing prognosis?

One of the most delicate and challenging parts of a medical oncologist's work is having conversations with patients regarding prognosis, especially in cases of terminal illnesses. Emotional intelligence, empathy, and clarity must all be balanced in these conversations. Hiring managers therefore want to be sure you can provide accurate and pertinent information while handling these difficult conversations with professionalism and compassion.

Sample Answer: It takes empathy and delicacy to discuss prognosis with a terminally ill patient. I think it's important to be supportive but also honest. It's critical to give them accurate information about their condition, available treatments, and possible outcomes.

But it's also important to frame the conversation in a way that keeps hope alive. This may entail concentrating on palliative care alternatives, quality of life, or even clinical trials.

It is important to adjust communication to the emotional and cognitive states of the recipient. While some patients may prefer broad outlines, others may require detailed information.

Making sure they feel knowledgeable, supported, and involved in their care decisions is the aim.

21.

How do you deal with the emotional toll that treating cancer patients can have on you?

Given the nature of the disease and the frequently intense relationships doctors develop with their patients, a career in oncology can be emotionally taxing. This is a question posed by potential employers to find out how you manage your emotional well-being in this demanding industry. They want to make sure you have healthy coping strategies in place so you don't burn out and can keep giving your patients excellent care.

Sample Answer: Empathy and self-care must be balanced to manage the emotional toll of working with cancer patients. To provide individualized care, I put a lot of effort into actively listening to my patients to understand their worries and fears.

To prevent emotional exhaustion, it's equally crucial to uphold personal boundaries. To control my stress levels, I regularly participate in physical activity and employ mindfulness practices like meditation.

And last, peer support is priceless. Colleagues can provide fresh insights on navigating challenging circumstances and provide emotional exhaustion relief by exchanging experiences and tactics.

22.

Could you give an example of a situation in which you had to work with other experts to treat a patient?

Collaboration is the cornerstone of medical oncology. Cancer treatment frequently necessitates a multidisciplinary approach involving experts from various fields. This test is intended to evaluate your capacity for respectfully working with a diverse team, cooperating positively toward a common objective, and ultimately enhancing patient care. It also sheds light on your ability to solve problems and manage challenging situations.

Sample Answer: I was treating a patient with metastatic lung cancer in one complicated case. The patient also had serious cardiac problems, which added complexity to the treatment regimen.

Throughout the patient's chemotherapy, I worked closely with a cardiologist to manage her heart condition. To guarantee the best possible outcome for our patient, we had frequent conversations regarding dosage modifications and possible side effects.

The patient's quality of life was not only prolonged but also enhanced by this multidisciplinary approach. It strengthened my conviction that teamwork is essential to delivering all-encompassing care.

23.

In cases where a patient or their family denies the seriousness of the diagnosis, how do you intervene?

Strong communication skills, emotional intelligence, and medical knowledge are all necessary to navigate the emotionally turbulent waters of an oncology practice. It may complicate treatment plans and be detrimental to the patient's health when a patient or their family is in denial about a diagnosis. Interviewers want to know if you can deliver the best care possible for the patient while managing these challenging circumstances with tact, sensitivity, and professionalism.

Sample Answer: I think that in these kinds of circumstances, it's best to be honest but kind." A patient's and their family's complete understanding of the diagnosis, prognosis, and available treatments must be guaranteed.

When elucidating medical terms and their implications, I would speak simply. A social worker or counselor can offer more support if they're still in denial, so I might bring them in.

Remember that the goal is to provide them with all the information they need to successfully navigate this challenging journey, not to force them to accept it.

24.

What modifications have you made to your practice to accommodate palliative care?

You will frequently treat patients who are battling terminal illnesses in your role as an oncologist. Providing relief from the symptoms and stress of an illness is the main goal of palliative care, which is why it is imperative to incorporate it into your practice. The way you handle palliative care demonstrates your understanding of patient needs, empathy, and compassion—elements that hiring managers in the healthcare industry greatly appreciate.

Sample Answer: I must incorporate palliative care into my practice." Taking care of patients' emotional and psychological needs is just as important as controlling their symptoms.

Creating customized care plans has been a close collaboration between me and multidisciplinary teams. These consist of techniques for managing pain, counseling, and guiding conversations within the family about end-of-life matters.

Additionally, it has been observed that the prompt incorporation of palliative care can enhance life quality and in certain instances, increase chances of survival. As a result, I think it's crucial to introduce this aspect of care right away.

When providing palliative care, communication is essential. I guarantee candid communication regarding expectations, fears, and goals with patients and their families. As a result, their wishes are taken into account and their care is administered with dignity.

25.

Regarding the clinical trial you participated in, could you kindly share your experience?

The core of oncology is clinical trials. They provide hope for more effective therapies if not outright prevention. Hiring managers aim to assess your scientific curiosity, your capacity to advance the medical community's knowledge and your commitment to improving patient care by asking about your direct participation in clinical trials. Additionally, it's an opportunity to assess your comprehension of the legal requirements and ethical issues related to clinical trial administration.

Sample Answer: I worked with a team in a recent clinical trial to examine the effectiveness of a novel targeted treatment for non-small cell lung cancer. Five hundred patients participated in the trial at various locations.

I was responsible for managing the administration of treatment, keeping an eye on side effects, and choosing patients based on genetic biomarkers. In patients with particular mutations, we observed that the therapy markedly increased progression-free survival.

This event brought home how crucial personalized medicine is to the field of oncology. Furthermore, it emphasized that careful data collection and analysis are necessary to guarantee accurate results.

26.

How would you handle a patient who declines a suggested course of care?

Assessing your communication abilities, empathy, and regard for patient autonomy are the main purposes of this question. You will probably deal with patients who may refuse prescribed treatments for a variety of reasons as a medical oncologist. The goal of the interview process is for interviewers to ascertain that you can communicate the possible outcomes of these decisions effectively and handle these difficult situations with comprehension and respect.

Sample Answer: I think the most important thing is to make sure that there is honest and compassionate communication when a patient declines recommended treatment. I can speak directly to them if I understand their worries or anxieties.

If alternate therapies were available, I would offer them while highlighting the advantages and disadvantages of each. Their decision regarding their health must be well informed.

Family members or mental health specialists could be helpful to involve if the refusal doesn't go away. Respecting the autonomy of the patient is crucial, in the end.

27.

Could you kindly explain a situation where you had to decide on a patient's course of treatment?

When it comes to a patient's treatment plan, medical oncologists frequently have to make difficult decisions. Asking questions like this helps hiring managers learn more about your ability to make decisions, your understanding of medicine, and how you handle difficult and demanding circumstances. Your ability to make well-informed decisions, effectively communicate with patients and their families, and strike a balance between the clinical and emotional aspects of care are all key points of interest.

Sample Answer: A patient with advanced lung cancer who qualified for targeted therapy was the subject of one difficult case. She might not live as long as she would have liked due to the medication's serious adverse effects. Following a discussion with my team, I decided to include the patient in the decision-making process. All the options, with their possible advantages and disadvantages, were presented.

It was not an easy decision, but honoring the patient's autonomy is essential in healthcare. The patient opted for comfort care rather than aggressive treatment.

28.

How have your patient treatment plans benefited from the use of genetic testing?

As treatments are customized based on each patient's unique genetic composition, medical oncologists are at the forefront of precision medicine. This process is greatly aided by genetic testing, which can identify specific treatment options and offer a patient's cancer road map. Interviewers therefore seek to understand how you have implemented this innovative strategy in your practice, showcasing your dedication to providing individualized patient care.

Sample Answer: In my practice, I've identified specific mutations in patients' cancer cells through genetic testing. Targeted therapies, which may be less harmful and more effective than conventional treatments, can be chosen with this information in mind.

An EGFR inhibitor, for example, may be preferred over chemotherapy for patients with EGFR mutations in lung cancer. Parapariboside Inhibitors may also be advantageous for a patient with BRCA-mutant breast cancer.

In addition, predicting the likelihood of metastasis or recurrence, helps us customize our surveillance plans. More frequent imaging or blood tests may be advised for high-risk patients.

To provide individualized treatment, improve results, and reduce side effects, genetic testing is therefore essential.

29.

What is your approach to managing conflicts among coworkers regarding a patient's treatment regimen?

Because it probes your capacity to manage intricate professional relationships in the healthcare setting, this question is crucial. In medicine, especially oncology, difficult decisions with significant consequences are frequently made, and conflicts can occur. Interviewers look for evidence that you can respectfully listen to and express your own opinions while advocating for your own in the interest of giving patients the best care possible.

Sample Answer: Considering the complexity of patient care, disagreements are unavoidable in a clinical setting. I think it's important to keep lines of communication open and to respect different viewpoints when these kinds of situations come up.

I would bring up evidence-based medicine and our common objective of achieving the best possible outcome for the patient in our conversation with my colleague. It might be helpful to involve a third party, such as a multidisciplinary team or senior consultant if we are unable to agree.

Every choice should ultimately be based on what is best for the patient, backed by the most recent findings and recommendations.

30.

Could you tell us about a case you handled where the patient had an uncommon or rare condition?

Using this question, hiring managers can assess your aptitude for handling difficult and complex situations. You will encounter a range of patient cases in your career as a medical oncologist, some of which may be uncommon or uncommon. They are trying to learn more about your approach to problem-solving, critical thinking skills, and handling unforeseen challenges, so they are asking you about your experience with cases similar to these.

Sample Anwer: A patient with Waldenström's macroglobulinemia—a very uncommon kind of non-Hodgkin lymphoma—stands out among the cases. The problem was that because it was so uncommon, there were no established treatment guidelines.

Based on her genetic profile, we had to use a customized strategy that included targeted therapies in addition to chemotherapy. A special complication of this illness that we also had to manage was hyperviscosity syndrome.

The experience underscored how critical it is to provide personalized care and stay abreast of new developments in oncology research. Because we collaborated closely with pathologists and hematologists throughout the process, it also demonstrated the importance of multidisciplinary collaboration.

31.

When recommending a course of treatment, how can you be sure that you are taking the patient's unique situation into account?

The duties of an oncologist extend beyond merely making treatment recommendations and diagnosing illnesses. It involves giving patients comprehensive care that considers not only their physical health but also their psychological, social, and even financial situations. In this situation, recruiters want to be sure you have the patience, empathy, and communication skills to recognize these factors and take them into account when coming up with a treatment plan.

Sample Answer: It is essential to comprehend a patient's unique situation before recommending a successful course of treatment.

I always begin by asking the patient all the important questions regarding their finances, family, lifestyle, and work obligations. This clarifies for me how well they can handle specific treatments. Their emotional preparedness and mental health are also taken into account, as these can have a big impact on treatment adherence and results.

In addition, I work in conjunction with other medical specialists who are involved in the patient's care, like nurses, social workers, or psychologists, to obtain a comprehensive understanding of the patient's condition. I make sure that the suggested treatment plan is feasible and effective by incorporating all of this information to make sure it fits the patient's particular situation perfectly.

32.

How do you help patients deal with the side effects of chemotherapy?

The inquiry mirrors the actuality of oncology practice, where controlling chemotherapy side effects is just as crucial as the therapeutic intervention. Taking care of side effects maintains the treatment plan's continuity while also enhancing the patient's quality of life. Thus, the interviewer wants to know how skilled you are at handling these side effects and how you would guarantee your patients' safety while undergoing cancer treatment.

Sample Answer: Managing the side effects of chemotherapy requires a multidisciplinary approach." When it comes to matters of nutrition, I frequently work with dietitians, and when it comes to medication administration, with pharmacists.

We use antiemetics both before and following treatment to prevent nausea and vomiting.

Promoting moderate exercise and getting enough sleep can help with fatigue.

When necessary, dose modifications or different medications are used to treat neuropathy. When a patient is in pain, we use analgesics based on the WHO pain hierarchy. To manage emotional distress, psychological support is also essential. When necessary, we connect patients with psycho-oncologists or support groups.

Since each patient is different, strategies must be customized to meet their specific needs. The best possible symptom control is ensured by routine monitoring and reevaluation.

33.

In what ways have you contributed to patient or family education regarding cancer and its management?

A medical oncologist's role includes education as a crucial component. Receiving a cancer diagnosis can be very overwhelming for patients and their families. It is vitally important that you can reassure them, help them navigate their treatment plan, and translate complicated medical information into a language they can understand. This test is meant to evaluate your ability to communicate effectively and show compassion for patients and their families in this trying time.

Sample Answer: In my opinion, patient education plays a critical role in the management of cancer." Informational sessions have been held with me to go over the diagnosis, possible side effects of therapy, and the significance of continuing care.

Additionally, I advise patients to enquire to make sure they comprehend their circumstances completely.

I offer advice to family members on how to help their loved ones through this difficult time by providing them with emotional and physical support. I think the total result of cancer treatment can be greatly enhanced by an informed patient and a helpful family.

34.

What was the situation and how did you modify your communication style to meet the needs of the patient?

Working with patients who have different backgrounds, personalities, and levels of knowledge about their conditions is part of what it means to be a medical oncologist. To give each patient the best care possible, you must be able to modify your communication style to suit their needs. It enhances adherence to treatment plans, fosters trust, and lessens patient anxiety. This test is intended to evaluate your empathy and adaptability, two essential traits for a productive oncologist.

Sample Answer: I worked with a young child who had leukemia and was afraid of hospitals during my residency. I changed my tone of voice to something friendlier and more lighthearted to help him feel more at ease. I spoke to him in plain terms and with analogies he could understand, rather than using medical jargon. For example, I referred to chemotherapy as "superhero medicine," using it to battle the "bad guys" in his body. This improved the treatment atmosphere and lessened his anxiety. I learned how crucial it is to modify communication methods to meet the needs of each patient individually to provide effective care.

35.

In your conversations with patients and their families, how do you approach the end of life?

Part of the job description for a medical oncologist includes having tough talks. Approaching the matter with empathy, candor, and understanding is crucial when it comes time to talk about end-of-life care. Inquiring about your approach to these discussions will help prospective employers assess your ability to support patients and their families emotionally and provide important information.

Sample Answer: "End-of-life discussions," which call for clarity, honesty, and empathy. Understanding the patient's condition, prognosis, and awareness of it is the first step I take in having these conversations. I then see to it that the conversation takes place in a quiet, cozy space. Family members offer emotional support and aid in decision-making, so it is imperative to include them if the patient gives consent.

In communicating the situation, I use straightforward, non-medical language and emphasize quality of life over the remaining time. Concerning end-of-life care, I urge patients and their families to voice their worries, fears, and desires.

As I provide all the information and emotional support needed, my job is to guide rather than dictate decisions throughout this process.

36.

What encounters with multidisciplinary cancer conferences have you had?

Oncology is no different from the rest of the medical community in that it values teamwork. An important component of this collaboration is multidisciplinary cancer conferences or tumor boards. Your track record in these types of settings can tell a lot about your capacity for teamwork. Professionals from a variety of specialties come together at these conferences to talk about treatment plans and patient cases. That's why prospective employers are very interested in your ability to contribute to these discussions.

Sample Answer: Multidisciplinary cancer conferences, or MCCs, are a really useful tool for patient care, in my opinion. Experts from different disciplines can work together on these platforms to create all-encompassing treatment programs.

Personalized therapies that take into account all facets of the patient's condition have resulted from these conversations, in my experience. Patient satisfaction and results have increased with this strategy.

But to make sure that everyone involved in MCCs knows their roles in the plan, it's also crucial to maintain effective communication and clear documentation during the meetings.

37.

Could you give an example of an instance in which you had to speak up in favor of a patient receiving a specific course of treatment?

Hiring managers can evaluate your abilities in patient advocacy by asking you this question. You are expected to be your patients' advocate in addition to providing medical oncologist care, especially when it comes to guiding them through complicated treatment options and helping them make healthcare decisions. You can demonstrate your knowledge of the healthcare system, your ability to negotiate, and your commitment to patient care by answering this question.

Sample Answer: I once had a patient with advanced lung cancer who was not improving with standard chemotherapy," as an example. Upon examining his case and the most recent research, I thought immunotherapy might be helpful.

Because this treatment was more costly and had not yet been proven to be the first line of treatment for his condition, his insurance company initially refused to cover it.

I decided to file an appeal because I had strong feelings about my patient's possible advantages. In support of the use of immunotherapy in cases similar to mine, I supplied comprehensive medical documentation and recent research. The patient started the new treatment plan after the insurance company ultimately changed its mind. His acknowledgment of our efforts to advocate for this course of action was encouraging.

38.

What steps do you take when a patient's cultural beliefs run counter to the suggested course of treatment?

I practice medicine in the real world. Treating patients with varying cultural backgrounds and their unique views on health and recovery presents challenges for oncologists. It's critical to show that you can respectfully consult with the patient's cultural beliefs and effectively communicate and negotiate treatment plans. Your ability to deliver patient-centered care, which is essential to contemporary healthcare, is demonstrated by this.

Sample Answer: I give patient-centered care a priority in these circumstances." When describing the advantages of the suggested treatment plan, it is important to acknowledge and honor the patient's cultural beliefs.

My opinion is that it is beneficial to involve a cultural liaison or interpreter in the event of a conflict, someone who can help to reconcile cultural norms and medical advice.

Even if this means coming up with a treatment plan that compromises or diverges from their beliefs, my ultimate objective is to make sure that patients are well-informed about their health decisions.

39.

Let me know which case you found most difficult and why.

Managing the complexities of each patient's condition is another one of a medical oncologist's duties in addition to treating them. Your ability to solve problems, your knowledge of medicine, and your stress tolerance are evaluated by answering a question about your most difficult case. It offers valuable perspectives on how you interact with other medical professionals and how you convey information to patients and their families in trying circumstances.

Sample Answer: An instance of a highly demanding case I managed involved a patient suffering from metastatic lung cancer, who had become resistant to initial treatment. To minimize side effects and preserve quality of life, managing the disease's progression was complex.

Understanding molecular oncology, precision medicine, and palliative care in their entirety was necessary for this case. Proficiency in communication was also required to have an honest and compassionate discussion with the patient's family about treatment options and prognosis.

The need for personalized, comprehensive patient care in oncology, as well as the significance of keeping up with changing research, were both highlighted by this case.

40.

What is the method by which you inform and involve the patient's family during treatment?

Managing emotionally charged situations and complicated medical information is a common aspect of an oncologist's work. Since patients' families are frequently just as involved in their care as the patients themselves, being able to effectively convey this information to them is a crucial aspect of the job. Your ability to manage these delicate conversations and keep families informed and involved is something that interviewers look for in candidates.

Sample Answer: To keep a patient's family informed and involved, open communication is essential. Before going over possible treatments, their advantages, disadvantages, and side effects, I usually begin by clearly stating the diagnosis.
I provide the family resources for more understanding and welcome their questions at every

turn. It is also essential to provide regular updates on the patient's condition.

The family's worries can be allayed and they will feel like they are on this journey if they are included in the decision-making processes. Respecting the patient's privacy and wishes while cultivating trust, empathy, and transparency is the key.

41.

How do you respond when a patient's insurance refuses to pay for a suggested course of care?

In the field of healthcare, insurance, and money concerns can have a direct influence on a patient's available treatments. As a medical oncologist, you might frequently encounter circumstances in which a patient's insurance does not cover the best course of care. The interviewer is interested in learning how you handle these challenging situations by striking a balance between the practical limitations of insurance coverage and the need for efficient treatment.

Sample Answer: My first course of action is to talk with the patient when a recommended treatment isn't covered by their insurance. They must comprehend their medical condition and the reasons this treatment is required, in my opinion.

I then consult the social workers or financial counselors at our hospital. They can assist in looking into alternate sources of funding like grants, installment plans, or charitable care initiatives.

Finally, I think about other worthwhile procedures that their insurance might pay for. My constant goal is to find an approachable solution without sacrificing the standard of care because patient care is of the utmost importance.

42.

Could you describe your encounter with a patient whose cancer treatment was significantly impacted by a significant comorbidity?

As with most medical specialties, oncology is not always an easy one to navigate. Numerous patients experience comorbidities, which can have a major impact on how they are treated for cancer. Interviewers can learn more about your ability to modify treatment plans to suit the specific needs of each patient, how you manage challenging medical circumstances, and how you interact with patients regarding their available treatment options by asking you this question.

Sample Answer: I worked with a patient who had severe COPD and lung cancer. Because the comorbidity could exacerbate respiratory symptoms, standard chemotherapy administration presented difficulties.

We took a customized approach, choosing targeted therapy that was less likely to exacerbate the COPD. Optimal management of both conditions was ensured through regular communication with the pulmonologist.

The management of patients with significant comorbidities necessitates individualized treatment plans and interdisciplinary teamwork, as demonstrated by this case.

43.

How have you kept up to date on new medications and therapies for cancer?

Being up to date on the latest advancements in cancer therapies and treatments is expected of oncologists. Since patients are entrusting you with their lives, you must be up to date on the latest developments in the field and able to assist them in making decisions regarding their care. Employers aim to assess your proactive approach to staying current in your field and your dedication to lifelong learning by posing this question.

Sample Answer: Oncologists must stay current with new medications and therapies for cancer. To stay up to date on the most recent research findings, I frequently read medical journals like The New England Journal of Medicine and The Lancet Oncology.

I also take part in webinars, seminars, and professional conferences where experts talk about cutting-edge treatment methods.

In addition, participating in professional networks such as the American Society of Clinical Oncology facilitates idea-sharing and knowledge-sharing among peers. Working with pharmaceutical reps also gives you access to information about new medications. This multifaceted strategy guarantees that I am knowledgeable about the most recent advancements in cancer treatment.

44.

How do you respond when a patient's religious convictions run counter to the suggested course of care?

The medical field requires a careful balancing act between emotional intelligence and professional expertise. You will probably come across patients whose religious beliefs may conflict with the treatment you are suggesting when dealing with life-threatening illnesses like cancer. Employing managers are looking for evidence that you can handle these delicate situations, honor the patient's beliefs, and deliver the highest caliber of care.

Sample Answer: I think a patient-centered approach is best in these kinds of situations. Respecting the patient's beliefs and having an honest conversation about their concerns is essential. I would give all the information required about the treatment plan, including its advantages, disadvantages, and any available alternatives. This aids patients in making knowledgeable choices.

Involving a hospital chaplain or a religious leader from the patient's community may be helpful if there is still conflict. They can assist in bridging the gaps between religious beliefs and medical advice. In the end, it comes down to striking a balance between honoring the patient's autonomy and giving them the best treatment possible within those constraints.

45.

Can you recall a situation in which you had to decide quickly on a patient's course of care?

The core of an oncologist's work frequently entails making important choices under pressure. Every patient is different, and occasionally their health can change drastically. Hiring managers use this question to assess your ability to think quickly on your feet, make deft decisions, and control risk when faced with an emergency. They want proof that you can remain composed under duress and still choose what's best for your patients.

Sample Answer: I had a patient with metastatic lung cancer who suffered from shortness of breath and severe chest pain all of a sudden during the night shift. The symptoms could also be the result of a tumor growing, but the EKG suggested a possible myocardial infarction.

I decided to treat both conditions at the same time, setting up an urgent CT scan and giving nitroglycerine and low-dose aspirin. Rather than showing signs of cardiac involvement, the scan revealed a pulmonary embolism. We initiated anticoagulation therapy right away. Making this choice allowed us to effectively manage the patient's condition without wasting any important time.

46.

How would you react if a patient asked you to try anything else—anything—when you had nothing left to give?

In medicine, you may simply run out of options, solutions, ideas, or hope at times. Everything has a limit, from the lowest level of hemoglobin that can be reached while still supplying oxygen to tissues to the point at which malignant tissue overtakes healthy tissue. This inquiry seeks to understand how you give up in a field where it is expected of you to never give up or give in.

Sample Answer: Upon creating a protocol, especially for a patient, I go over it all with them, from the hopeful start to all the potential outcomes—both good and bad. By the time we get to the point of surrender, I would go over it again, just like we did at the beginning, so that the timeline in arrears could demonstrate that everything that could be done has been done. I would reassure the patient that I am here for any "positive" surprises that may arise as well as for any end-of-life decisions they would like to make.

Even though it is depressing, it is my duty as a professional who has witnessed this desperation numerous times to keep my patient grounded in reality. At this point, I would presume that the patient and their family had come to terms with this fact and that my duties might need to change from being devoted to faking our demise to being committed to upholding the ultimate dignity of a life well-lived.

47.

Would you set up a referral for a hysterectomy and ovarian excision as a preventative measure for an 18-year-old nulliparous woman who has a strong family history of ovarian cancer?

It appears that this question is an attempt to gauge how cautious you would be to avoid taking shortcuts when it comes to significant and contentious issues. If there is any protocol, you can't go wrong citing it; if not, you can't go wrong enlisting the assistance of others who are better qualified to make such decisions, particularly when the problem is more significant than you (which it is).

Sample Answer: I would assemble a multidisciplinary team that included her primary care physician, social worker, psychologist, ethicist, and me. If we worked together, I'm sure we could properly guide her toward making such a significant life choice.

I'm the oncologist, so in the end, I'm the one who can help her understand the risks involved in doing nothing. I would, however, welcome her parents to participate in the conversation as they are neither 0% nor 100%. Furthermore, her childbearing is not the only thing at risk here; there may be many children, grandchildren, the family legacy, and other things as well. Furthermore, even in cases of high-risk genetics, malignancy rarely starts at this age, so I would suggest that we establish a surveillance protocol just for her, allowing us to take prompt action if needed."

48.

What would you do if a patient experienced a bad reaction as a result of a prescription error?

It is easier to endure the consequences of being honest than it is to weather the consequences of being dishonest. Take ownership of it. Physicians are required by most hospitals or state boards to complete online courses regarding medication errors and the precautions that should be taken in their charting protocols to reduce the likelihood that they will occur. Therefore, your response should focus on prevention techniques, fact admission, and harm reversal. It's also always a good idea to tell the interviewer that you have never experienced it, so don't be afraid to say that.

Sample Answer: Since patients entrust us with their care, mistakes—while regrettable—fall under the purview of whatever professionalism standard is upheld. This kind of maintenance entails reviewing all of my decisions and orders twice and thinking of potential problems all the time. If that doesn't work, I can't let my patient down by being dishonest in any way. As part of my professional responsibilities, I would then apologize to the patient and level with them if I had caused any harm.

My first duty is to treat the adverse reaction—which could be caused by an overdose, an allergic reaction, or the incorrect medication—to "undo" the harm. I should then tell the patient what transpired and the actions I thought were required to lessen the harm.

I've never had it happen to me, but I know what to do because we've all received training on it, and I would abide by hospital policy. I would take care of any response that the error had caused, record the error and the actions I took to fix it, and fully explain to the patient what had happened, how it had happened, and any potential repercussions. I would then hope that the patient-doctor relationship could withstand such a sincere error.

49.

How may you assist our group?

Employers use this question to find out if you are aware of the position for which you are applying and whether you did any research on the role to prepare for the interview. It's critical to demonstrate in your response that you have done your homework on the oncology practice and the position. In a similar vein, you should go over the practice's philosophy of patient care, available treatments, and how you fit in.

Sample Answer: I spoke with a friend who knows your group and looked up your practice online before our meeting. I saw that while you have many doctors who specialize in ovarian cancer, there aren't many that concentrate on lymphomas. This gives me hope that I can put my training to use and advance the treatment of lymphoma patients. Despite this, I also talk about cancer.

50.

Could you describe the perfect practice environment or circumstance?

The purpose of this inquiry is to learn more about your preferences regarding location. This covers the number of patients seen, call coverage, and the offices and hospitals that the oncology practice covers. Your response to the query demonstrates your work ethic and readiness to contribute to the practice's growth as a team member. You can also express your preference and understanding of the differences between the hospital, community-based, academic, and private practice employment models. Your response must highlight your dedication to the clinic and its clients.

Sample Answer: I know I have to put in a lot of effort to advance my career and practice. It's also critical that I use creative brand-building strategies, like peer-to-peer gatherings and community discussions, to promote the team among referring physicians. I also recognize the value of taking advantage of the hospital's physician lounge. My goal is to cultivate connections throughout the network and position myself as a dependable and compassionate medical professional.

51.

How many patients a day do you feel comfortable seeing?

This is a test of your willingness to work hard and be a team player from the interviewer. In your response, demonstrate that you recognize the value of being accessible to provide care for every patient in the oncology practice. Rather than giving a figure for the number of patients you can see each day, make sure your response demonstrates your understanding of oncology's economics.

Sample Answer: I am aware that the oncology field faces reimbursement pressures, and that productivity, efficiency, and quality of care are critical to success. I am also aware of how crucial it is to be accessible to provide care for any patients that the practice sends my way. I'm ready to put in a lot of effort and work quickly while still giving my patients excellent care. As I gain more self-assurance in my work, I hope to effectively contribute to the group's accomplishments.

52.

What are your professional aspirations?

This question is used by the interviewer to find out how you plan to use the job to further your career and personal development. You can outline your immediate and long-term professional objectives along with your plan for achieving them. It's also helpful to show how the job helps you reach your career objectives. For instance, you might have plans to expand your oncology practice.

Sample Answer: I have always wanted to establish my ontology practice to combat ovarian cancer. I therefore plan to use this job to further my professional, administrative, and medical expertise in the field of oncology practice. Additionally, the job gives me the chance to build strong working relationships with my fellow oncologists, who may end up being crucial partners in the practice.

Bonus

20 Interview tips

1. Investigate the Company: Look beyond the website of the business. Examine recent press releases, news stories, and social media posts to learn about the organization's accomplishments, ongoing initiatives, and potential difficulties. With this comprehensive understanding, you can confidently discuss how your experiences and skill set complement the objectives of the organization.
2. Recognize the job description: Divide the job description into its most important duties and requirements. Think of concrete instances from your prior experiences that show how you fulfill each requirement. This thorough comprehension aids you in expressing during the interview why you are a good fit for the position.
3. Practice Frequently Asked Interview Questions: Get ready to answer frequently asked questions, such as "Tell me about

yourself," "What are your strengths and weaknesses," and "Why should we hire you?" Make sure your responses are clear, concise, and captivating by practicing in front of a mirror or with a friend.

4. Emphasize Your Successes: Make a list of all the things you have accomplished professionally, emphasizing measurable outcomes. Talk about the good things you did in addition to what you did. Employers can see concrete examples of your contributions from this evidence-based approach.

5. Showcasing Your Soft Skills: Determine the essential soft skills needed for the position, such as teamwork, communication, and flexibility. Give particular examples of these abilities from past positions. Talk about a collaborative project that worked well or an instance where you had to be flexible to get past a difficult situation.

6. Get your questions ready: Formulate inquiries that genuinely reflect your interest in the position and the company. Inquiring about possible future projects, company culture, or team dynamics are a few examples. In addition to demonstrating your interest,

thoughtful questions assist you in determining whether the organization aligns well with your professional objectives.

7. Dress Appropriately: Make sure your outfit matches the industry norms and the company's dress code. If in doubt, go with something a little more formal. You can show that you respect the company and the interview process by dressing professionally.

8. Get There Early: Make sure to factor in any delays when planning your route to the interview location. Being early for the interview gives you time to gather your thoughts, go over the essential points, and enter the room looking composed. It also shows that you are dependable and dedicated to being on time.

9. Body Language Is Important: Keep an eye on your body language the entire time. Keep your head up, sit up straight, and give a solid handshake. Nonverbal clues project professionalism and confidence, which enhance your overall impression of the interviewer.

10. Prepare to Talk About Your Weaknesses: Prioritize your efforts to improve the areas

where you have made efforts to strengthen your weaknesses. Talk about specific measures you've taken to overcome obstacles, highlighting your dedication to career development. This shows self-awareness, an eagerness to learn, and the capacity to transform setbacks into learning experiences.

11. Be Enthusiastic: Share your excitement for the position by talking about the particular facets of it that thrill you. Tell about how your qualifications and experiences complement the chances and challenges this job offers. Contagious enthusiasm can make a good, lasting impression on the interviewer.

12. Flexibility and Issue-Solving: Give instances where you proved to be flexible and capable of solving problems. Talk about how you overcame difficult situations or handled changes at work. Candidates who can think quickly on their feet and adapt well to changing conditions are highly valued by employers.

13. Mirror the Company's Values: Make sure your answers reflect the main principles of the organization. Emphasize how your actions align with the organization's culture

by sharing examples of when your actions demonstrated similar values. The interviewer will know that you are likely to succeed in the company's work environment if this alignment is present.

14. Describe Your Long-Term Objectives: Describe your professional goals and how this role fits into your overall career path. Highlight your dedication to lifelong learning and growth, demonstrating how the position fits into your long-term objectives and advances your professional development as a whole.

15. Keep It Brief and Targeted: During simulated interviews, practice answering questions succinctly and precisely. Steer clear of side topics and extraneous details. Make sure your main points are understandable and straightforward for the interviewer to follow by presenting your material in an organized way. This exhibits proficient communication abilities.

16. Handle Tense Situations: Give examples of how you've handled tension in the work environment. Talk about the techniques you use to remain composed under duress, make

wise choices, and have a positive outlook. Candidates who can handle difficult situations calmly are highly valued by employers.

17. Investigate the Interviewers: Find out about the experiences and responsibilities of the people interviewing with you. Make sure your answers speak to their particular interests or areas of expertise. This tailored approach demonstrates that you have taken the time to learn about the dynamics within the team.

18. Tell About Your Educational Experiences: Talk about times you overcame a challenging learning curve to successfully pick up new skills. Emphasize your flexibility and dedication to continued professional growth. Candidates who embrace learning opportunities and strive for continual improvement are highly valued by employers.

19. Remain Upbeat: Remain upbeat during the interview, even when talking about difficulties. Pay attention to the answers and the things you can learn from trying circumstances. Being positive is a desirable

trait that can help create a positive impression and demonstrate resiliency in the face of difficulties.

20. Observation Following the Interview: After the interview, send a personalized thank-you email no later than 24 hours. Thank you for the chance, restate your interest in the role, and briefly describe how you think your qualifications meet the needs of the company. Your professionalism and excitement are further supported by this post-interview correspondence.

www.ingramcontent.com/pod-product-compliance
Lightning Source LLC
Chambersburg PA
CBHW062323290526
45794CB00005B/1873